STO
✓

FRIE W9-DIZ-130
OF ACPL

CO. SCHOOLS

GIANTS, DRAGONS,
AND GODS

Books by DIRK GRINGHUIS

TULIP TIME
YOUNG VOYAGEUR
ROCK OIL TO ROCKETS
BIG DIG
BIG HUNT
OF CABBAGES AND CATTLE
SADDLE THE STORM
IN SCARLET AND BLUE
OF SHIPS AND FISH AND FISHERMEN
FROM TALL TIMBER
MYSTERY AT SKULL CASTLE
OPEN DOOR TO THE GREAT LAKES
STARS ON THE CEILING
GIANTS, DRAGONS, AND GODS

Written and illustrated by

DIRK GRINGHUIS

MEREDITH PRESS   *NEW YORK*

GIANTS, DRAGONS, AND GODS

Constellations and Their Folklore

Text and illustrations copyright © 1968 by Dirk Gringhuis. All rights reserved. No part of this book in excess of five hundred words may be reproduced in any form without permission in writing from the publisher. First edition.

Library of Congress
Catalog Card Number 68-15203

Manufactured in the United States of America for Meredith Press

CO. SCHOOLS
C686'796

FOR THE DUCHESS ELÉNA

PREFACE

In this book are several of the interesting legends that the ancients made up to explain the star constellations. Of their forty-eight constellations, the stories of twelve major ones are included here, as well as legends from the American Indian, the Eskimo, and the Australian bushman, and from ancient India, Persia, and other folk cultures. Very little space is given to modern scientific thought. This can be presented better in books devoted to our universe. Instead, the intention of this book is to remind us of other star watchers in other times and places. For those who are fortunate enough to be in an area unaffected by city lights, with the clear star-studded sky above at night, these stories can have real meaning. For others, today's modern planetariums always offer a clear sky and star stories to go with it.

D. G.

CONTENTS

GIANTS, DRAGONS,
AND GODS

GIANTS, DRAGONS, AND GODS

Where did the stories of the constellations start? Who first saw the star shapes and gave them names? Because no one really knows, we can only call these first people the star watchers. History does tell us that later the ancient astronomers recorded forty-eight constellations. Today, in spite of some changes in boundaries, these constellations still look very much the same as when the first star watchers saw them.

Since then, from time to time, other constellations have been added. Most of them are below the equator in southern skies, and are stars that we cannot see in this latitude. But altogether, astronomers list eighty-eight. Your position on earth (latitude and longitude), the weather conditions, the time of night and the time of year, all decide which of them you can see and where.

As for the star stories themselves, there are many ideas about how they may have begun. Some people think that early man, standing at his cave door, or herders tending their flocks may have watched the heavens and imagined animals, heroes, or monsters in the night sky. These were figures taken from folklore to help identify certain constellations.

But why should so many myths from so many parts of the world be so much alike? How could simple shepherds possibly have constructed the zodiac, those twelve constellations lying along the apparent path of the sun, moon, and planets? Perhaps the ancients knew more about nature than we think. Perhaps the star plotters were early priests, the pictures religious symbols. In any case, figures were used. There were animals like the bull, ram, horse, lion, bear, dog, and whale, birds like the dove, eagle, and raven, such objects as ships, a scale, cup and crown, and lyre, and even fish and a crab. There were imaginary dragons and sea monsters, and men and women, kings, queens, and heroes were there as well—wrestling, fighting, hunting.

Some of the star watchers were called astrologers. These men claimed to be able to foretell the future from the stars. Even today there are people who follow astrology and its horoscopes, charts, and forecasts, which are based on the movements of the signs of the zodiac. The term *sign,* as used in astrology, is not the same as the term *constellation*. The signs were placed in twelve equal divisions along the imaginary path of the sun, or *ecliptic*. To people in the ancient world these signs overlay the constellation bearing the same name. Due to the movement of the earth, this is no longer true, and as time goes on, they will move even farther apart.

The zodiac begins at the point where the sun crosses the celestial equator in the spring. This is the vernal, or spring, equinox, when the sun is in the sign of Aries.

The *equinox* is the time when nights and days are equal in length. People who live on the equator always experience days and nights of twelve hours each, but on either side of the equator days and nights are not equal, due to the earth's rotation and the apparent path of the sun. During most of the year, the farther one is from the equator, the greater the difference in length between day and night, but there are times, twice a year, when day and night are both twelve hours long everywhere on earth. This is during the vernal equinox and during the autumn, or autumnal, equinox.

Aries the Ram is the first sign the sun seems to pass through on the zodiac. After Aries come Taurus the Bull, Gemini the Twins, Cancer the Crab, Leo the Lion, Virgo the Virgin, and Libra the Scale, the sign for the autumnal equinox. Next come Scorpio the Scorpion, Sagittarius the Archer, Capricorn the Goat, Aquarius the Water Bearer, and Pisces the Fish.

Thirty-six constellations, twenty-one to the north and fifteen to the south, lie on either side of the ecliptic, which is the circle made by the earth's orbit around the

sun. As the constellations of the zodiac circle close to this orbit, it appears as though the sun, moon, and planets were moving against the background of constellations. The sun also appears to move through the zodiac after sunset and before sunrise.

By carefully observing these movements, ancient astronomers, star watchers who believed the stars governed man's destiny, in such places as Babylonia were able to predict the seasons. From this knowledge came the belief by astrologers that the stars affected our lives. They tried to work out complicated charts showing when a certain constellation would be near a certain planet. For example, from these charts, which gave each person a sign of the zodiac according to his birth date, they made up horoscopes predicting that person's future.

Today's scientists and astronomers find no truth in the beliefs of the astrologers, who were attempting "to explain the unexplainable."

This same urge, however, has brought to us many myths and folktales. Generally the myths were told for two reasons. The first was to answer questions, such as, "How was the world made? How will it end?"

The second reason was to explain the social order of the time and to record special events and customs. Because people enjoy hearing about the mysterious unknown, stories that once may have recorded everyday happenings became, as they were told and retold, something quite unusual, even unbelievable or supernatural.

Today we call a collection of tales made up by a single people that people's folklore. And strangely enough, tales told by such widely separated peoples as the American Indians and the Greeks may have a great deal in common.

Many tales were religious. For example the story of a king who actually lived may, in folklore, become the story of a god. This is as true in legends from the South Seas or from the Aztecs of old Mexico as it is among the Germans, Irish, Russians, Chinese, or Eskimos.

In these tales dragons, giants, heroes, and gods appear. Belief in dragons may have come from early worship of the snake. When four legs, like a crocodile's or a turtle's, were added, and when the snake's darting forked tongue was changed into a tongue of fire, a dragon was born. Giants may have simply been taller invaders, or heroes who grew in height as their legends grew.

It is these legends, transformed into the night skies, that are the stories of the constellations.

TWINS IN THE SKY

Long ago in the ancient Greek city of Sparta lived two brothers, the twin sons of King Tyndareus and his queen Leda. Spartan youths were well known for their strength and bravery, and the twins, Pollux and Castor, were no exception. Pollux was a champion boxer and runner, Castor an excellent horseman, able to ride and tame the wildest mounts. Both enjoyed games and tests of strength. But most of all the brothers loved each other, even though mighty Zeus had given Pollux the gift of immortality while allowing Castor to remain a mortal.

One day, seeking adventure, Castor and Pollux de-

cided to join the crew of the vessel *Argo*, which was
about to set sail in search of the Golden Fleece. Jason,
the *Argo's* captain, was delighted to have the brothers
aboard, as were his men, who were called the Argo-
nauts. Setting sail, they encountered rough weather,
which turned into a roaring gale. As they wallowed
in the heavy seas, the crew cried out to Orpheus the
Musician to touch his lyre and calm the terrible waves.
Suddenly, out of the wind-torn sky, twin lights appeared over the heads of Castor and Pollux. Some of the
men thought they were stars; others saw them as twin
fires. At the same moment, as suddenly as it had come,
the storm ceased. Ever since that time these twin fires,
called St. Elmo's fire, have meant fair weather for
seafarers.

After returning safely with the Golden Fleece, Castor
and Pollux set out on another mission, this time to find
and drive out the pirates lurking in the Hellespont, the
straits that separate Europe and Asia Minor. The brothers were again successful, and when they returned at
last, the seas were safe once more for travelers.

By now seamen throughout Greece and the ancient
world were saying that the twins were special friends
of the god Poseidon, and shipbuilders began placing the
sign of the twins on the prows of their vessels.

Then, as young men will, the brothers fell in love.
Unfortunately the girls, the nieces of Tyndareus, were
already betrothed, and the men to whom they were
engaged became angry and challenged the brothers to
combat. A great battle took place. At its end the rivals

of Castor and Pollux were dead, but Castor, too, had fallen, mortally wounded.

Pollux, knowing himself to be immortal, was torn with grief, and prayed to Jupiter that he and his brother not be separated. Either he, Pollux, must share death with his brother, or Castor must be brought back to life. Touched by the request, Zeus willed that the brothers should share both death and immortality. So both of them lived for a time after that and then they died and dwelt in the infernal regions. Later they were taken by the father of the gods and placed in the heavens for all the world to see, an example of love and devotion.

Today the twins can still be seen very clearly in the early evening at the beginning of winter in our hemisphere. The constellation, which rises in the eastern sky, is named Gemini.

This Greek tale of twins and the twin stars is only one of many legends handed down to us from the ancients. Other countries and peoples had their twins as well. The Egyptians told of Horus the Elder and Horus the Younger. Sometimes the twin stars were called the Sprouting Plants because when they appeared at night it was spring in Egyptian skies and the time of growing things. Ancient star maps show Gemini as two brothers with the stars, Castor and Pollux, at their heads, just like the St. Elmo's fire that marked them on the voyage of the *Argo*.

In Peru, old charts picture them either as twins or as

a pile of bricks, for in many parts of the world the two were thought of as the first builders of cities.

Among the Eskimos, the constellation took the form of the two door blocks at the entrance of an igloo.

Star watchers of India named them the Twin Horsemen. Among the Arabs, they were the Two Peacocks. Australian bushmen called them the Young Men.

Today if you wish to see Gemini, first locate Ursa Major, the Big Dipper or the Great Bear. Run an imaginary line from the star at the far tip of the handle to the star at the base of the dipper. Carry this line about one and a half times farther and you will arrive at the brightest of the twins, Pollux. Quite close to him is Castor, almost as brilliant.

BEARS IN THE SKY

Every twenty-four hours the earth turns and the skies seem to swing overhead. To people living north of the equator, the stars at the north pole, which are called the circumpolar constellations, are always in view, endlessly circling the pole. The stars at the equator seem to rise and set.

Polar constellations are at about forty degrees north latitude. Most of them are important, for from them we can locate other constellations, the way we use the Big Dipper to point out Gemini.

Northern circumpolar constellations are: the Big Dipper (Ursa Major or the Great Bear), the Little

Dipper (Ursa Minor or the Little Bear), Cassiopeia (the Queen), Cepheus (the King), and Draco (the Dragon).

Perhaps the best known are the Bears, big and little. Among the Greeks there was a legend about them.

Far below the heights of cloud covering Mount Olympus, the forest lay at peace. Birds sang, leaves rustled, and in a sun-speckled clearing a doe and her fawn drank at a swift stream. Now and then they raised wet muzzles and gazed at the forest's edge.

All at once the doe stiffened, ears up. Something was moving in the underbrush. She whirled on tiny hooves, her soft eyes white-rimmed. A twig cracked and from the trees stepped mighty Zeus in human form.

Instantly the doe was off in great bounds, her fawn close behind. As she disappeared, Zeus raised his head, listening. A sound of sweet singing came floating down from the tree-covered hills. Stepping back into the shadows, the god waited. The singing grew louder, and then into the clearing stepped a slender, beautiful girl. On her flowing hair rested a garland of leaves that exactly matched the soft green garment she wore.

As Zeus stepped forward and gently greeted her, the girl, startled, put her hand to her throat and gazed up at him with soft eyes.

"Forgive me, goddess of the forest," said Zeus, "but I stayed to hear your song."

The girl dropped her eyes. "I am no goddess, sir, but

only a hamadryad, a nymph called Callisto, who follows the huntress Artemis."

Zeus sighed. "You are as beautiful as she is," he said.

Every day after that Zeus left his golden throne high on the mountain and went to the forest clearing to meet Callisto. Finally, his wife, the tall and beautiful Hera, became suspicious. Mounting her chariot drawn by peacocks, she followed her husband at a distance and saw him with the nymph. In anger she drove back to Olympus, determined to punish the girl.

Two days later, on a morning when Zeus began a journey to another part of the earth, Hera's chance came. Once more she called for her chariot, and when Callisto came singing into the clearing, she found, instead of the handsome stranger, a tall queen whose eyes flashed in anger.

In terror, Callisto realized what she had done. This could be none other than the goddess Hera. The stranger must have been Zeus, king of the gods!

Trembling, she sank to her knees.

"So you dared to seek the love of the husband of Hera," said the queen haughtily.

"Forgive me, mighty Hera," answered the nymph tearfully. "I did not know him."

"Who are you?" demanded the queen.

"They call me Callisto. I live in the forest with my small son Arcas."

"Then you are the nymph from the train of Artemis." Hera paused.

Hopefully Callisto raised her head.

But the queen's smile was cruel. Stretching out her hand, Hera pointed a finger at the trembling girl. "I, Hera, decree that hereafter you shall dwell in the forest as before, not as a temptress, but as a beast. Instead of following the huntress you shall be the hunted!"

Pleadingly, Callisto lifted her hands, only to see that they were already covered with thick brown hair. As she watched in horror, her dainty nails became sharp claws. She tried to cry out, but her soft voice had become the whining of a beast. Staggering to her feet, she stumbled into the woods, then dropped to all fours and ran. The wood nymph had become a bear.

On she ran, heading for her home and her small son. When she reached the hut she saw Arcas playing with a baby rabbit near the doorway.

Rising on her hind legs, Callisto held her arms out toward the lad, whining pitifully. But Arcas saw only a shaggy bear reaching for him. He screamed, then went dashing off down the path. Behind him, Callisto's brokenhearted cries sounded like the growls of a bear.

For days she waited, hoping that Zeus might return and set her free. But although the god knew of her plight, he dared not further anger his wife. Instead he waited, keeping an eye on both the bear and her small son.

As the days passed into months and years, Callisto lived as a bear. Seldom did she catch sight of her son growing tall and straight among the other nymphs. At sixteen, Arcas was strong and well formed. He was expert with the bow and arrow, and loved to run,

wrestle, and throw the javelin. Then one day, when he was old enough to hunt alone, he set out into the forest with his javelin determined to return with a trophy of his own.

As he rounded a bend in the forest trail, he saw straight ahead of him a bear which, upon seeing him, rose on its hind legs with paws outstretched. Arcas hesitated. There was something familiar about the animal.

With a soft growl the bear started forward. Instantly the boy raised his javelin and drew back his arm. Then, with a cry, he dropped the weapon and gazed at his hands. He too was turning into a bear. In the next instant a mighty hand reached down from Olympus. Seizing both bears by the tails, Zeus lifted mother and son high above the earth and placed them in the heavens.

That night and every night thereafter, they trudged their slow circle around the pole—bears with long tails stretched by Zeus's hand, guiding travelers far below.

Ursa Major and Minor are probably among the oldest of the known star groups. Strangely enough, the term "bear" seems to have been used by a great number of people, even though it takes a great deal of imagination to see a bear, particularly a long-tailed one, in the sky.

That the ancient Greeks should have left this story, and a similar one was told by the American Indians, is one of those remarkable events that take place in folklore. However, the bear has always been a favorite

subject with storytellers, perhaps because a bear standing on its hind legs looks very much like a man. But
whether the animal is a trained circus bear, a giant
Alaskan brown bear in a zoo, or an imaginary one from
the story of Goldilocks, he has qualities of both humor
and power, which men have always admired.

Not all countries knew the bear, of course. In some
places the constellation had other names. The Egyptians called it the Dog of Set. Sometimes it was the
Chariot. In France and England it was called The Wain,
or wagon, in Scandinavian countries The Great Wagon,
in Poland The Heavenly Wain. In India it was de-
scribed as The Seven Bulls or The Seven Bears.

As for the seven stars in the constellation, Benetnasch
at the handle's end is called Alkaid in Arabic, meaning
Chief Mourner. The next, Mizar, means Girdle of Cloth.
The third is Alioth, meaning Sheep's Tail, and Megrez,
which connects the handle to the bowl, is called Root
of the Tail. At the bowl's far side is Dubhe, or Back
of the Bear. This star was very important to the ancients. In 5100 B.C., the temple of Hathor at Dendera
was built so that Dubhe's rays would pierce a long
passage and fall upon the figure of the goddess inside.

At the dipper's bottom is Merak, The Beast's Loin.
Merak and Dubhe are the pointers for Polaris. The last
star is Phad (Phecda), meaning Thigh.

Among most American Indian tribes, the bear is the
favorite theme for this constellation. The four stars of
the dipper are the bear, while the three in the handle
become the hunters. Among the Iroquois, the first hunter

carries a bow, the second a kettle, represented by a
faint star next to the middle hunter, and the third fire
sticks.

In autumn, the first hunter shoots an arrow into the
bear and the blood flowing from the wound turns the
autumn foliage red.

The Eskimos of Point Barrow had the same legend.
However, some Eskimos think of Ursa Major as four
men carrying a dead man. This same legend appears in
Arabian legends, hence the name "Chief Mourner" for
Alkaid.

One of the most interesting legends is told by the
Zuñi Indians, who live far enough south to watch the
Bear set below the horizon. To them this means the
bear has gone into her den to sleep, and the time marks
the coming of winter. Now the ice gods are free to
wander the land and man must huddle close to his fire.

When at last the bear awakens, cold and hungry, she
smells her enemies, the ice gods, outside her den. She
growls her anger and is answered by thunder. The ice
gods tremble and finally flee to their caves in the north.
It is spring once more.

The Cree Indians of western Canada have a legend
in which the constellations are called the Big and Little
Dipper. The legend has in it many of the elements
found in all folklore—taboos, snakes, and violence.

Somewhere in the beginning of time, says the legend,
there lived a man, his woman, and their two sons, one
of them half-grown, the other very small.

The family lived in a wigwam of many poles, which

C686796

was covered with mud for warmth, and they were happy living off the land. Then one day the father, Nota, noticed that his wife was behaving strangely. Instead of tending the lodge fire, she often went into the bush land after wood, which she did not need. Curious, Nota followed her and was surprised at her unusual gait as she went up to a certain place. There, beside a rotten tree, she stopped. Kneeling down, she began tapping on the ground beside a small hole. Suddenly, to Nota's surprise, many snakes came out of the hole and crawled around the woman, who sat down and began playing with them.

Angry, Nota decided to punish her for this evil thing. The next day he went hunting, but no animal did he kill until he found a moose. Instead of skinning it, he returned to the wigwam and told his wife to go and get it.

A woman must not disobey her husband—this is the law—but the wife tried to make her journey shorter by throwing a long strip of meat in the fire. Nota saw the meat becoming shorter as it burned, seized it, and stretched it out again. Now he knew his wife was trying to use evil magic to shorten her journey.

After she was gone, he went to the place of the snakes and made the tapping sound, but as each snake appeared he cut off its head. At last, when only one small snake was left, he cursed it, saying it would always be small and easily conquered.

Nota then hurried back to his wigwam of many poles. He took out four things, and spoke to his elder son.

"You must leave with your brother and take these things I give you. This owl will make for you a fence of thorns, this flint is for fire, this rock is for changing into a mountain, this beaver tooth will make a mighty river. Evil has come because of your mother. You must now go and bring back good to our land and our people."

"And where will you be, Father?" asked the young man.

"Look to the northern sky, my son," said his father. "There you shall see me."

And so the young men fled toward where the sun sleeps.

When the woman returned, she was angry to find her snakes dead and decided that she must kill her husband in return. But as she came through the opening in the wigwam, her husband was waiting. In one stroke, he cut off her head.

As her head rolled away, it said to her body, "Chase him into the sky; I will go after the sons."

To this day the Great Dipper can be seen in the northern sky. It is the form of Nota. Near it is the Little Dipper, which is the wife's body. But she dare not approach her husband for fear of the guardian North Star.

Today these constellations are commonly called the Big and Little Dippers. On clear nights the seven bright stars form the shape of the Big Dipper, a long-handled, flat-bottomed container for dipping up water. The two stars marking the bottom side of the dipper are called the pointers. They point to the constant star Polaris, which is set in the handle of the Little Dipper. Sometimes, depending on the hour of the night and the season of the year, the constellations appear to be upside down. As this heavenly clock swings counterclockwise around Polaris, experienced sky watchers, by careful observation, can tell the time.

THE KNEELER'S
TWELVE TASKS

Among the major constellations found to the north on a spring evening are not only the Great Bear and Little Bear, but Castor and Pollux of Gemini, Boötes, Lyra, Cepheus, Cassiopeia, Perseus, Taurus, Auriga, and Hercules.

One of the most stirring stories is that of Hercules, daring hero of many legends. A mortal, he was still the son of Zeus, and even as a child showed great courage. When Hera, who was not his mother, became jealous once again of Zeus's fondness for mortals, she sent two great serpents to destroy Hercules in his cradle. But the infant seized the serpents and strangled them and so saved himself and his twin brother.

From that day on Hercules was known for his strength and courage. As he grew he learned many skills from the great teachers of the day. Pollux taught him boxing, a son of Poseidon taught him to use the bow, and Linus, a son of Apollo, taught him to play the lyre. From Autolycus he learned wrestling and from Chiron the art of healing.

When he became a man, Hercules married Megara, daughter of King Creon of Thebes. The marriage was a happy one, and at first it seemed as though Hera had forgotten him. But this was not the case. In a fit of anger, Hera drove Hercules mad, and during his madness he killed his wife and children, believing them to be his enemies.

After he recovered his senses, Hercules was haunted by what he had done, and asked help against Hera's vengeance from the Oracle at Delphi. The high priestess told him to go to his cousin Eurystheus, there to bind himself for eight years as servant to his cousin and to fulfill all tasks given him. In return he would receive eventual immortality.

Now King Eurystheus was a suspicious and cowardly king. Fearing that Hercules might claim his throne, to which he had a right, the king gave him ten dangerous and seemingly impossible tasks. When they were done, Eurystheus discounted two of the tasks and gave Hercules two more. These tasks became known as the Twelve Labors of Hercules.

When Hercules was successful at his first task, which was to find and kill the Nemean lion, the disappointed king then ordered him to kill the nine-headed monster Hydra. Again Hercules triumphed.

Hercules' next mission was to kill the terrible wild boar in the mountains of Erymanthia. By the time Hercules had killed the boar the king was beside himself with fear and anger, so he sent him to capture the stag sacred to Artemis, the Goddess of the Hunt. Wind-swift and capable of trampling its pursuers into dust, the stag proved difficult; it took Hercules nearly a year to run the animal down and capture it in a thicket.

Next he faced the man-eating Stymphalian birds in the swamps of Arcadia. These monsters had beaks and talons of brass which could pierce the strongest armor. Undaunted, Hercules killed most of them, and the rest fled. Then he went to sea, on the king's orders, this time to kill the mad bull of Crete. After that he captured the wild, man-eating mares of Diomedes.

Now another labor awaited Hercules. Far beyond the Black Sea lived a king named Geryon, who was very rich and owned many oxen. Geryon was a three-headed monster, and Hercules' task was to steal a thousand oxen for King Eurystheus from under the watchful eyes of Geryon. But two years later Hercules was back, and with him were a thousand of the finest oxen.

The next labor was of a more delicate nature. Ordered to seize the jeweled belt of Hippolyte, queen of the warlike Amazon women, he found himself ac-

cused of an attempted kidnapping. Angered and suspecting treachery, he slew Hippolyte.

Now, in near desperation, the king sent him for some of the golden apples from the tree sacred to Hera, Hercules' old enemy. For many years he wandered, seeking this tree, until finally a serpent led him to the sacred fruit which, when eaten, gave a mortal immortality.

However, his next task was even more dangerous, for now he had to descend into the realm of the dead and bring back the three-headed dog Cerberus, who guarded the gates of Hades. Using the tricks that Pollux had taught him about animals, Hercules made friends with the dog and brought him back safely.

And now there was but one task left. Hoping to delay him again for many years, the king sent Hercules to clean the stables of King Augeas, one of the richest men in the world. Among his riches were 12,000 oxen, which were bedded in stables that had not been cleaned for thirty years. Weary now of the impossible tasks that had been put in his way, Hercules was determined to finish this one as soon as possible. By changing the course of the river, he forced it to flow through the stables and cleaned them in a single day.

At last, with the twelve labors done, Hera's curse was ended. But still Hercules could not find peace. His second wife, jealous of the nymphs who admired her husband, tricked him into putting on a poisoned robe. Knowing the end was near, mighty Hercules climbed to the top of Mount Oeta and there built his own funeral pyre. Lying down upon it, his great club beside him, he ordered the pyre to be lighted. But at the last moment Zeus, in pity and admiration, transported Hercules by golden chariot into the night sky.

If you look north in the evening sky, you will see the constellation today as a large group of faint stars. Six of the brightest form a butterfly or *H* shape below Corona Borealis. This ancient group of stars was well known hundreds of years before the age of Hercules. Sometimes it was called The Kneeling One or The Phantom. Usually the figure is shown holding a club in his right hand, while in his left he holds a branch with twined serpents or a branch with the golden apples. But he always kneels with one foot on the constellation of Draco the dragon. In his head is the star Alpha, or Ras Algethi, meaning Head of the Kneeler in Arabic.

As for the Twelve Labors of Hercules, the old star religion placed some of them according to the sun's path through the zodiac: first the Nemean lion, or Leo, then Virgo, then Taurus, representing the thousand oxen, and finally his last labors. The capture of the golden apples is symbolized by the guardian dragon, Draco, and the three-headed dog, Cerberus, is represented by the three animals of Gemini—the two bears and Canis Major, the Great Dog.

LEO THE KING

Looking south in the spring, you will see a single constellation, Leo the Lion, riding almost directly overhead. In February this same sickle-shaped constellation rises in the east during the early evening.

In November a shower of meteors, called Leonids, comes from the constellation of Leo.

Leo contains the star Regulus, the brightest star in the southeast in the spring. In ancient times Regulus was thought to be the ruler of the heavens. Other names for it were the Lion's Heart and the Star of Kings.

Regulus is a giant white sun, 5 times the size of our sun, and 250 times as bright. Astrologers thought it had

great powers of good or of violence depending on its
position in relation to other heavenly bodies.

In Greek mythology Leo was the ferocious Nemean
lion sought by Hercules as the first of his twelve labors.
Hercules was told by the terrified people in the foot-
hills of the Nemean Mountains that every night the
beast stopped at a certain pool to drink and then came
down to spread havoc in the villages.

Hercules hid himself beside the pool and waited, a
steel-tipped arrow ready in his bow and a long sword
loosed and ready at his side.

As the sun set, something came padding down the
path from the mountains above. Then a huge body
moved out into the clearing. It was the Nemean lion,
black-maned and terrible, with eyes of yellow fire.
Slowly the animal king moved toward the pool and low-
ered his head to drink.

Hercules drew back the silent bowstring. Straight toward the lion's shoulder the arrow flew. But instead of
piercing the bulging muscles and finding the heart, it
fell harmlessly to the ground.

Flinging down his bow, Hercules drew his sword and
lunged at the snarling beast. Swinging the weapon in a
gleaming arc, he aimed for the lion's mighty head. But
the blade was torn from his hand. With a deafening
roar, the lion reared straight up, claws seeking the belly
of his enemy. But Hercules dodged beneath the slash-
ing paws and, seizing a nearby tree, tore it from the
ground and turned in time to meet the lion's charge.
Using the tree as a club, he brought it down across the

snarling face with all his might. For an instant the lion hesitated, and in that instant, Hercules sprang straight across the lion's back. His powerful arms encircled the shaggy throat and held on, tighter and tighter, until at last the yellow eyes glazed and closed.

Hercules removed the hide from the dead lion and wrapped himself in its weapon-stopping armor. Taking up his club, he strode off into the morning.

The lion has long been known in Asia, Greece, and Egypt, and everywhere he has represented majesty and power. Lion fountains were common in the ancient world. The Tribe of Judah used the lion as their symbol. In ancient Persia the sun and the lion appeared on the national banner. Mexicans worshiped the lion, and in Peru the cougar became the lion symbol.

THE BOASTFUL QUEEN

Among the constellations in the northern sky in the spring is Cassiopeia, which is shaped like a chair or a throne. Queen Cassiopeia, legend tells us, was part of a royal family in the ancient kingdom of Ethiopia. Her husband was King Cepheus, their daughter the lovely Andromeda. Andromeda was so lovely, in fact, that her mother could not help but boast of her beauty to all who would listen. Finally, she even boasted that her daughter was more beautiful than the Nereids, who were in the court of the immortal sea god, Poseidon.

A guest overheard the boast and hurried to the seashore, where she found the cliff house of the Nereids.

When the pearl-clothed nymphs came through the sea-weed curtains, she told them of Cassiopeia's boast.

Angered, the nymphs plunged into the sea and swam to Poseidon's palace. Here they called out for revenge on this mortal who had made such a foolish boast. Poseidon listened and agreed that Cassiopeia had indeed spoken out of turn, as mortals were sometimes prone to do. But the Nereids were determined on revenge. Finally, unable to stand against the clamor of fifty nymphs, Poseidon agreed to avenge them. Picking up his trident, he directed all sorts of disasters to fall upon the lands of King Cepheus.

The next morning poor King Cepheus found his fields blighted, his rivers dry, his land a barren waste. Bewildered, he sent a messenger to the shrine of Zeus asking what wrong he had done. The messenger returned with the news of his queen's folly and of Poseidon's wrath.

Trembling, the king asked how he could escape further disaster. Weeping openly now, the messenger told him what must be done. Andromeda herself must be sacrificed by being chained to the rocks on the coast until a sea monster, Cetus, came to devour her.

Next morning a sad procession moved slowly toward the sea. The beautiful Andromeda, pale but determined to save her people, waited while great chains were fastened around her slim wrists and ankles. Then, kissing her weeping parents good-bye, she lay back on the rocks to await her fate.

Alone, she watched the sun rise in the sky and for

the last time saw the white-capped waves, the deep-
blue horizon, and the whirling sea birds. Then suddenly
the sea parted. A huge greenish back, covered with
great shining scales, appeared for an instant, then disappeared. Andromeda bit her lips to keep from crying
out. One second passed, and another. Then, not fifty
feet in front of her, rose up a terrible monster whose
wide jaws, filled with rows and rows of teeth, dripped
seaweed and slime. Terrified, the poor girl flung her
head backward, trying to escape the monster moving
toward her. As she did so, a strange shadow passed
over her. Thinking it was a bird, she glanced sideways.
But instead of a bird hovering there she saw a handsome young man flying through the air. (Some people
say he was riding the winged horse Pegasus). In his
right hand he waved a glistening curved sword, in his
left a shield. At his belt he carried what looked like a
heavy bag or sack. As he swooped lower, she saw small
wings on his feet.

Landing on the rocks, the young man bent down
over the chained maiden.

"Why are you captive here?" he asked.

And through her tears Andromeda poured out her
story.

"You shall not be devoured, beautiful princess," said
the young man, and he leaped high into the air. Up,
up, he went. Then he turned and, thrusting his sword
into his belt and at the same time protecting his eyes
with his polished shield, he reached into the sack.

"Andromeda!" he shouted. "Close your eyes tightly until I give you the word to open them!"

Andromeda closed her lids instantly and turned her head away.

Finally the voice said, "Now open them."

Not daring to hope, Andromeda slowly looked toward the place where the monster waited. But instead of the horrible grinning mouth and the slime-covered scales, she saw a monster turned to stone.

Again the youth alighted on the rocks and, with two quick sweeps of his curved sword, he cut the chains that bound the helpless princess.

Suddenly from the cliff overlooking the sea came shouts of joy. Cepheus, Cassiopeia, and the whole court raced toward their princess, weeping with happiness.

Then Cepheus stepped forward and placed his hand on the young man's shoulder. "Who are you, and what can we do to reward your bravery?" he asked.

"I am Perseus. With the help of the gods I have conquered the snake-haired Medusa, whose head I keep in this sack. The sight of that head turns anyone who looks at it into stone. It was with its help that I rescued Andromeda."

"And the reward?"

Perseus, smiling, reached out his hand toward the beautiful princess. "Your daughter for my wife," he said softly.

Perseus and Andromeda lived happily together for many years. Two sons and two daughters were born to them. Perseus and Andromeda, and Cepheus and Cas-

siopeia as well, were taken up to the skies to dwell forever among the constellations when they died. Even Cetus the sea monster found a place among the stars.

Second only to the Great Bear, Cassiopeia is one of the most conspicuous constellations in the northern sky. To find her, draw an imaginary line to Polaris from any of the stars in the Dipper's handle. Then, from Polaris, continue until you come to the chair, which is a W-shaped constellation of five stars.

Legend says, however, that although Queen Cassiopeia was placed among the sky's immortals, the Nereids still had their revenge. Being a circumpolar constellation, the bragging queen must spend part of her time every year sitting in an undignified position upside down.

PLOWMAN
IN THE SKY

All heroes among the constellations were not warriors.
One such who found himself among the stars was
Boötes.

Son of Demeter, Goddess of the Harvest, Boötes had
a younger brother, Plutus; both of them were mortals.
Plutus was jealous of his elder brother's inheritance of
lands and herds and raised an army to drive Boötes
from his palace.

Boötes disliked violence, so rather than try to reclaim
his property, he decided to become a man of the soil
and to make his living with his hands. Taking only two
of his oxen, he found himself a small field and built a
house there.

In those days farmers had few tools with which to work. The only way to break up the soil and form rows for planting was for a man to drag a curved stick through a field.

One day while working his land Boötes stopped to wipe the perspiration from his head and happened to glance at the grazing oxen. He envied them their muscled flanks and heavy shoulders. That night in his hut he began to think of ways in which the oxen might pull the curved stick through the furrows instead of the man. Using small pieces of string and slivers of wood, Boötes made tiny models. It was dawn by the time he finished, but instead of going to bed he rushed outside and began to fashion a full-size piece of curved wood. Then he cleverly tied ropes on the patient oxen and fastened them to his new invention.

Meanwhile Demeter, his mother, had learned of Plutus' treachery. She hurried to her eldest son, expecting him to be nursing his wounds and planning revenge. Instead she saw a field filled with long straight rows and, at one corner of it, Boötes, his oxen, and his wonderful plow.

As Goddess of the Harvest, Demeter was delighted. Embracing her son and praising his cleverness, she offered him her aid.

Boötes smiled. Wiping the dust from his face, he looked out over the field that he had plowed in a single day. Stretching out his arm, he pointed to other fields as yet unplowed.

"My mother," he said, "I was not born to wage war

or rule men. All I ask is that I be allowed to remain a farmer and that you bless my fields so that they may prove fertile."

Demeter nodded happily. "You are wise, my son. And the time will come when farmers shall bless your name for the gift you have given them."

After many years of rich harvest, Hermes the Messenger came to lead Boötes to the land of the dead. But Zeus instead took him up in a white cloud and placed him among the immortals, where to this day he drives his plow on warm summer nights.

During the spring and summer Boötes is one of the chief constellations. The Plowman has a kitelike form, with the great star Arcturus in its tail. It lies between Virgo the Virgin and the Big Dipper, and is followed by the Northern Crown (Corona Borealis) and Hercules.

Boötes' figure is shown in several ways, but generally it is that of a running man holding a staff or a spear in one hand and the leashes to his oxen in the other, although some people say the leashes are fastened to hunting dogs pursuing the Great Bear. The Arabs thought of Boötes as a shepherd with his faithful sheep dogs. These dogs form the more modern constellation of Canes Venatici, which lies just beneath the Great Bear. Boötes is also thought of as a herdsmen guiding the Wain, or wagon, as the Big Dipper is sometimes called.

In any case, this constellation, containing Arcturus, one of the brightest stars, still follows its unending path year by year in a great circle around the pole.

THE DOG
AND THE GIANT

So far in the stories animals have been ferocious, and enemies of man. However, there was one faithful friend, Canis Major, the dog of the giant hunter, Orion. His name was Sirius and he led the hounds for his master.

At one point in Orion's adventures, the giant was blinded and carried to a forsaken seashore. Separated from his master, Sirius waited, not knowing of the tragedy. Finally he could wait no longer and set out across the island of Chios looking for Orion. Day after day he traveled, stopping only to drink at a stream. His great body grew thin, his throat raw from baying

without an answering call. At last he picked up the scent of his beloved hunter. Nose to ground, he followed it across the meadows and through the woods until it ended at the impassable sea.

Meanwhile, Orion, blind and helpless on the shore to which he had been carried, heard the distant sound of a hammer. Knowing it to be the hammer of Cyclops, helper to the god Hephaestus (Vulcan), he strode into the sea. Following the sound, the giant—for he was a giant even though a mortal—reached the island of Lemnos, where Hephaestus had his forge. There the god had pity on him and, loaning Orion a small Cyclops as a guide, sent him to the eastern edge of the world to the palace of Apollo. Here the powerful rays from the mighty Apollo restored his sight.

Instead of returning to his old hunting grounds, Orion left for warmer lands. On the Island of Crete, this handsome hunter met the beautiful Goddess of the Hunt, Artemis, who welcomed him as a part of her train.

When Apollo saw his sister with a mortal, he grew angry. In vain he pleaded with her to give up Orion. Artemis refused. Then one day, as Orion was walking on the bottom of the sea, Apollo, the all-seeing one, saw the top of the giant's head rising out of the water. Turning to his sister, whose eyesight he knew could never equal his, he taunted her.

"You claim to be an archer," he said. "Let us see you send an arrow into that gleaming rock far out to sea."

The huntress tossed her curls, raised her bow, and

sent an arrow arching high over the sea straight into the target. The dark spot disappeared.

That evening Orion's body was washed ashore with the arrow still lodged in his great head. In remorse and in an effort to ease Artemis' grief, Apollo set Orion in the sky. As a final favor, Artemis asked that Sirius, the faithful dog of whom Orion had spoken, be placed there too at his master's feet.

Sirius is the brightest star in the constellation of Canis Major, and also the brightest star in the entire sky. There are many legends about this giant Dog Star. The Egyptians worshiped it and built temples to it. Each year they looked for its appearance, for then they knew it was time for the Nile to flood and time for a new harvest. Its appearance became a sign of good fortune and also of watchfulness, for when the star rose in the east early in the morning, it was time to move their goods to high ground. And so Sirius the faithful was not only a watchdog but a bearer of good tidings.

THE STAR PATH

In addition to the forty-eight constellations of the ancients, there are many so-called modern ones. The naming of some of these constellations actually dates back as far as the first century, although most of them are of seventeenth-century origin. While some of these constellations are found in northern skies, most of them are seen below the equator, either hidden from our sight or close to the southern horizon.

A fairly recent constellation is Canes Venatici, which represents the two hunting dogs of Boötes. Discovered by the astronomer Hevelius at the end of the seventeenth century, it lies just under the handle of the Big Dipper near Boötes.

While Canes Venatici is not a well-known constellation compared to the more familiar forty-eight, it still contains one of the finest star clusters known. It is thought to contain over fifty thousand stars, and some of the brightest of them are two thousand times brighter than our sun.

Another constellation, this time in the far north, is the Giraffe, or Camelopardalis. Long and fairly faint, it does have four bright stars, and fills a formerly thought vacant space near Perseus, Auriga the Charioteer, the Big and Little Dippers, and Cassiopeia.

One constellation that lies far to the south, close to the south pole, is Crux, the famous Southern Cross. Here on the Milky Way its four bright stars make the ragged but irregular figure of a cross standing upright.

At the foot of the cross is the brilliant Alpha Crucis. This star was thought by the astrologers of old to possess special powers toward the mysterious and the supernatural.

But no story of the stars could be complete without a reference to the path that covers more than a tenth of the sky. This bright arch, seen in the fall and the winter, is called the Milky Way.

Most of the legends refer to it as a pathway. The ancients thought it a highway of the gods, a path for the souls of the dead.

In China and Japan it became The Celestial River or sometimes The Yellow Road. The Egyptians thought it

was made up of grains of wheat thrown by the goddess Isis when she was pursued by a monster. Bushmen in faraway Australia say it was made by a girl from an early time who threw wood ashes into the sky. And far to the north some Eskimos also call it a trail of white ashes.

Among the Indians of North America the Milky Way was thought to be a pathway for souls climbing into heaven toward the Village of Souls awaiting them. Guarded by watchers who seized the wicked and cast them out, it also had campfires—the bright stars—which were built by the departed ones on their travels to the hereafter.

Ancient Greeks said it was The Road to the Palace of Heaven. The Romans called it The Milk Road and thought it was caused by the flood of milk on which the child Mercury was fed.

Other people called it a Stitch Where the Sky Was Sewn Together, or The Path of the Snake, or even The Path of Noah's Ark.

It took Galileo's telescope to prove that actually the Milky Way was the glow of many far-off stars. Photographs, taken through today's powerful telescopes, show that the stars number in the billions. When we look at the Milky Way, we are apparently looking down the long "tunnel" of our own galaxy at a huge cloud of stars. As the layers deepen, the stars seem more plentiful.

Our Milky Way galaxy, which includes the sun and the solar system and all the stars that can be seen by the naked eye or through a telescope, is shaped like a huge flat spiral. This giant wheels around its center, just as the planets revolve around the sun, with the stars closest to the center moving the fastest. Within this galaxy are clouds of cosmic dust as well as many star clusters, and beyond it, as shown by telescopes, exist other galaxies like it.

In the varying luminous band of the Milky Way are two dark spots called Coalsacks, one near the Southern Cross and one near the Northern Cross, which were a mystery to the ancients. They appear to be other galaxies or clouds of dust or gas called nebulae. If there are no stars nearby to light these nebulae, they seem to black out part of the Milky Way.

The legends in this book are only a few of the stories that people of the past made up to explain the stars and the constellations they form. Some of the stories date back to the ancients, some to primitive tribes, but all of them seem to have been an attempt to remember and name the stars that make up the night sky.

And those of us who are modern sky watchers can also share the thrill of the ancients as we watch a constellation reappear year after year and remember its story. For the world is an ever-changing place, and to find old friends in all seasons waiting to greet us can be a comforting and rewarding sight.

Key to Pronunciation

Tyndareus: tin-DARE-us
Leda: LEE-dah
Pollux: POLL-ux
Hamadryad: ham-a-DRY-ad
Alkaid: AL-cade
Mizar: MEE-zar
Megrez: MEG-rez
Dubhe: DOOB-he
Alioth: AL-ee-ot
Phad: FAAD
Dendera: DEN-der-ah
Eurystheus: yur-IS-thoos
Megara: MEG-a-ra

Nemean: NEE-mee-an
Erymanthia:
  eer-ee-man-THEE-a
Stymphalian: stym-PHAL-e-an
Cepheus: SEE-fus
Cassiopeia: cass-ee-o-PEE-a
Andromeda: an-DROM-e-da
Perseus: PER-SOOS
Nereid: NEER-ee-id
Ceres: SEER-ees
Boötes: bo-o-tees
Arcturus: arc-TOO-rus
Sirius: SEE-ree-us

A List of the Most Familiar Constellations

Ara, the Altar	A-ra
Andromeda	an-DROM-e-da
Aquarius, the Water Bearer	a-QUARE-ee-us
Aquila, the Eagle	a-QUEE-la
Aries, the Ram	ARE-ees
Auriga, the Charioteer	aur-EE-ga
Boötes, the Plowman	bo-o-tees
Camelopardalis, the Giraffe	camel-lo-PARD-al-is
Cancer, the Crab	CAN-cer
Canes Vanatici, the Hunting Dogs	CAN-es-ven-AT-i-sy
Canis Major, the Great Dog	CANE-us-MA-jor
Canis Minor, the Little Dog	CANE-us-MY-nor
Capricornus, the Goat	cap-ree-CORN-us
Cassiopeia, the Queen	cass-ee-o-PEE-a
Cepheus, the King	SEE-fus
Cetus, the Whale	SEE-tus
Coma Berenices, Berenice's Hair	co-ma-ber-en-EE-cees
Corona Australis, Southern Crown	co-RON-a-aus-TRA-lis
Corona Borealis, Northern Crown	co-RON-a-bor-ee-AL-is
Crater, the Cup	CRAY-ter
Corvus, the Crow	COR-vus
Cygnus, the Swan	SYG-nus
Delphinus, the Dolphin	del-FINN-us
Draco, the Dragon	DRAY-co
Equuleus, the Colt	EE-quel-us
Eridanus, the River Eridanus	er-REE-dan-us

Gemini, the Twins	JEM-in-i
Hercules	HER-cul-ees
Hydra, the Serpent	HI-dra
Lacerta, the Lizard	LA-ser-ta
Leo, the Lion	LEE-o
Leo Minor, the Little Lion	
Lepus, the Hare	LEE-pus
Libra, the Scales	LY-bra
Lupus, the Wolf	LOOP-us
Lynx	LINX
Lyra, the Lyre	LY-ra
Monoceros, the Unicorn	mo-no-SEER-os
Orion	or-I-on
Pegasus, the Flying Horse	PEG-a-sus
Perseus	PER-soos
Pisces, the Fishes	PY-sees
Puppis, the Stern of the Ship *Argo*	POO-pis
Sagitta, the Arrow	SAJ-it-ta
Sagittarius, the Archer	saj-it-TARE-ee-us
Scorpius, the Scorpion	SCOR-pee-us
Sculptor	SCULP-tor
Scutum, the Shield	SCU-tum
Serpens, the Serpent	SER-pens
Sextans, the Sextant	SEX-tans
Taurus, the Bull	TORE-us
Triangelum, the Triangle	tri-ANG-u-lum
Ursa Major, the Great Bear or Dipper	UR-sa
Ursa Minor, the Little Bear or Dipper	
Virgo, the Virgin	VIR-go